STATE PROFILES

CONNECTICUT

BY ALICIA Z. KLEPEIS

BELLWETHER MEDIA • MINNEAPOLIS, MN

Blastoff! Discovery launches a new mission: reading to learn. Filled with facts and features, each book offers you an exciting new world to explore!

BLASTOFF! UNIVERSE

BLASTOFF! Beginners — GRADE K

BLASTOFF! READERS — GRADES 1-3

BLASTOFF! DISCOVERY — GRADE 4

This edition first published in 2022 by Bellwether Media, Inc.

No part of this publication may be reproduced in whole or in part without written permission of the publisher.
For information regarding permission, write to Bellwether Media, Inc., Attention: Permissions Department,
6012 Blue Circle Drive, Minnetonka, MN 55343.

Library of Congress Cataloging-in-Publication Data

Names: Klepeis, Alicia, 1971- author.
Title: Connecticut / by Alicia Z. Klepeis.
Description: Minneapolis, MN : Bellwether Media, Inc., 2022. | Series: Blastoff! Discovery: State profiles | Includes bibliographical references and index. | Audience: Ages 7-13 | Audience: Grades 4-6 | Summary: "Engaging images accompany information about Connecticut. The combination of high-interest subject matter and narrative text is intended for students in grades 3 through 8"– Provided by publisher.
Identifiers: LCCN 2021019649 (print) | LCCN 2021019650 (ebook) | ISBN 9781644873786 (library binding) | ISBN 9781648341557 (ebook)
Subjects: LCSH: Connecticut–Juvenile literature.
Classification: LCC F94.3 .K586 2022 (print) | LCC F94.3 (ebook) | DDC 974.6–dc23
LC record available at https://lccn.loc.gov/2021019649
LC ebook record available at https://lccn.loc.gov/2021019650

Editor: Kate Moening   Designer: Brittany McIntosh

Printed in the United States of America, North Mankato, MN.

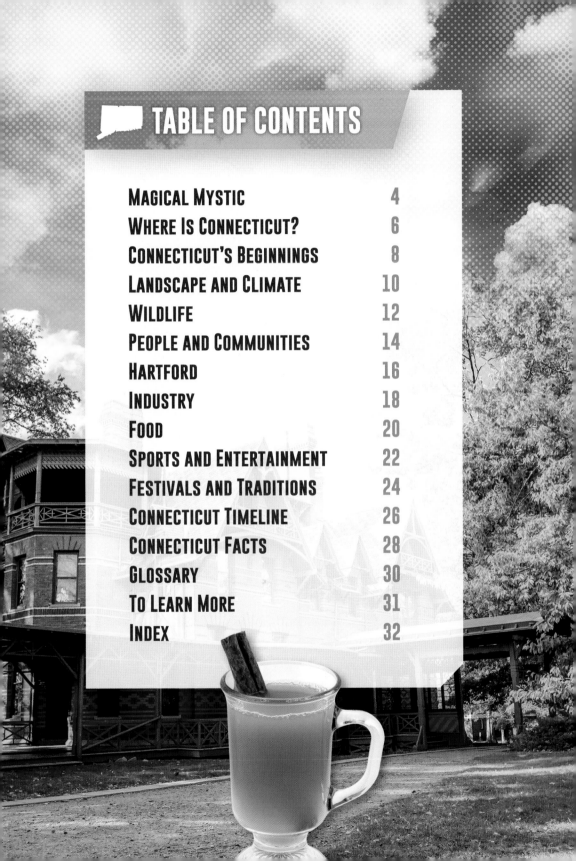

TABLE OF CONTENTS

A family arrives at the Mystic Seaport Museum in Mystic on a warm summer morning. A gull flies by on a salty breeze. The family begins the day exploring the *Charles W. Morgan*. This huge wooden whaling ship dates back to 1841! Next, the family heads to the Discovery Barn. They learn how to **furl** a sail and tie sailor knots.

CHARLES W. MORGAN

DINOSAUR STATE PARK

MARK TWAIN HOUSE & MUSEUM

SLEEPING GIANT STATE PARK

STEWART B. MCKINNEY NATIONAL WILDLIFE REFUGE

After eating seafood by the **marina**, the family heads to the Mystic Aquarium. They see harbor seals, African penguins, and beluga whales. After an ice cream, the family takes a sailboat ride around Mystic Harbor. Welcome to Connecticut!

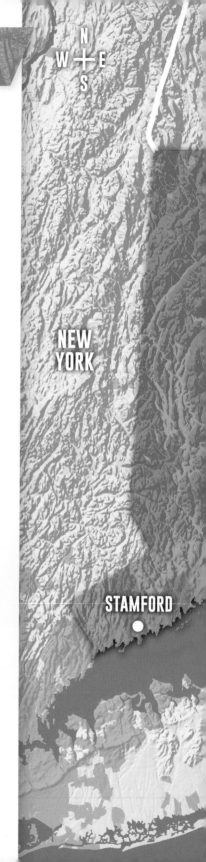

Connecticut is in the northeastern United States. It is part of **New England**. This rectangular state covers 5,543 square miles (14,356 square kilometers). Its capital, Hartford, is near the state's center. The Connecticut River runs through Hartford and divides the state in half. The biggest city, Bridgeport, lies in the southwest.

To the west of Connecticut is New York. Massachusetts sits to the north. Rhode Island forms Connecticut's eastern border. Long Island **Sound** lies south of Connecticut. This long body of water is connected to the Atlantic Ocean. It has both freshwater and saltwater!

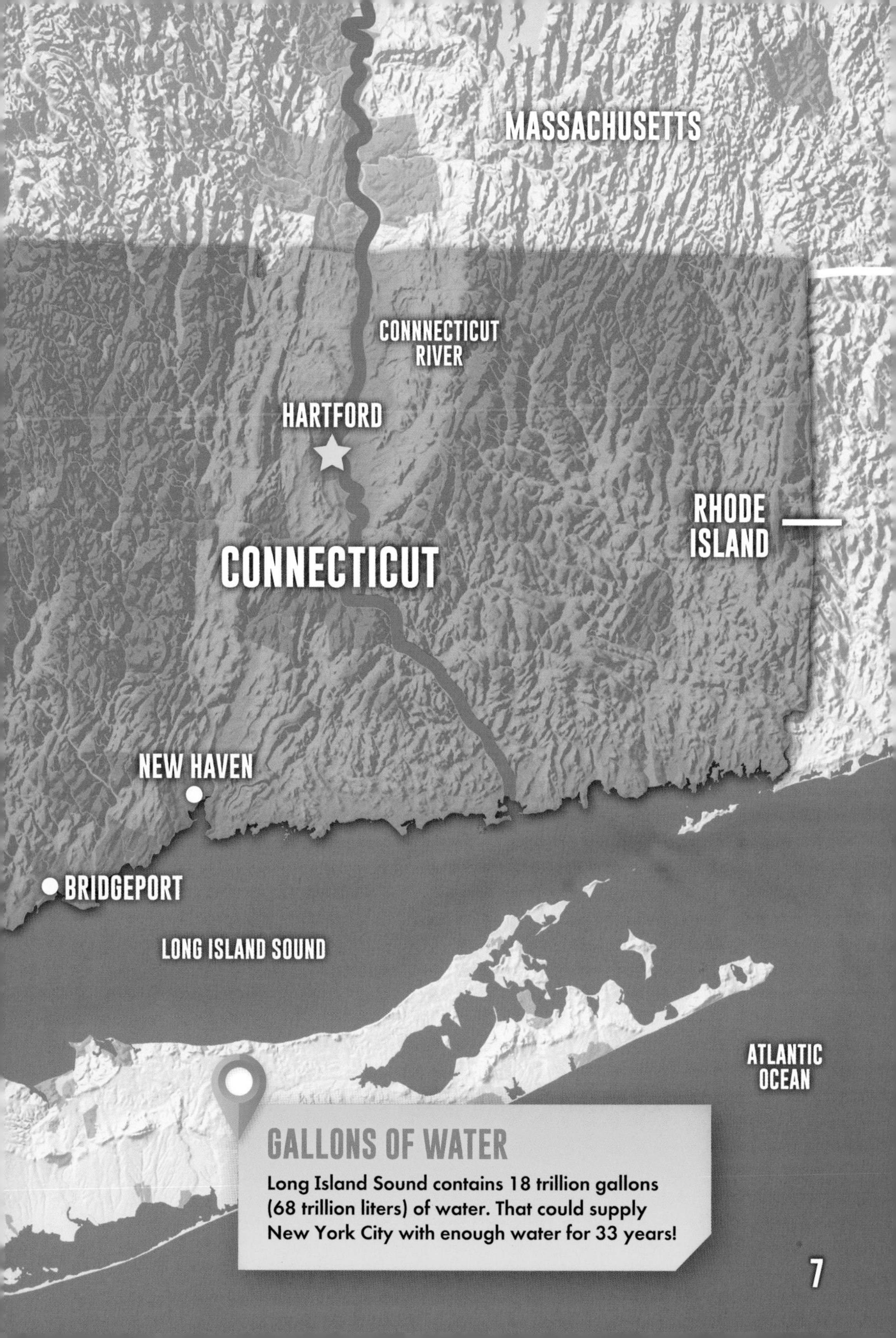

MASSACHUSETTS

CONNNECTICUT
RIVER

HARTFORD
★

CONNECTICUT

RHODE
ISLAND

NEW HAVEN
○

BRIDGEPORT
○

LONG ISLAND SOUND

ATLANTIC
OCEAN

GALLONS OF WATER

Long Island Sound contains 18 trillion gallons
(68 trillion liters) of water. That could supply
New York City with enough water for 33 years!

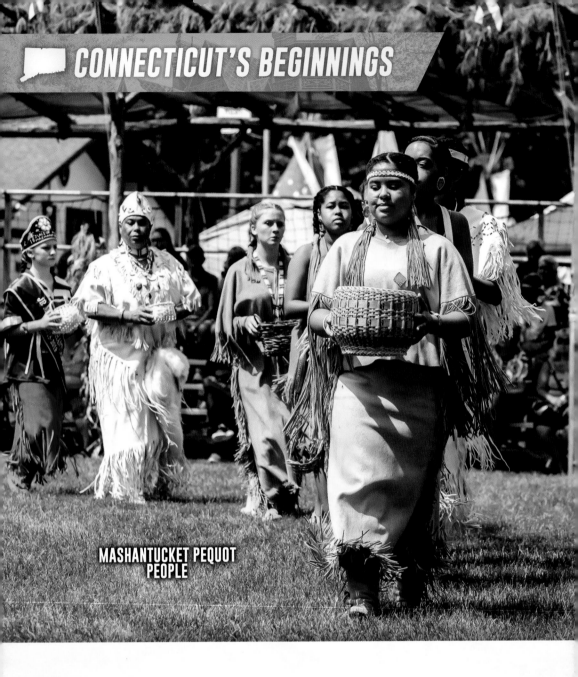

MASHANTUCKET PEQUOT
PEOPLE

People have lived in what is now Connecticut for more than 12,000 years. Eventually, about 16 separate Native American groups lived in the area. They included the Pequot, Mohegan, Niantic, Schaghticoke, and Paugussett peoples.

In 1614, a Dutch sailor named Adriaen Block was the first European to explore the area. English and Dutch **colonists** founded **settlements** in the early 1630s. Many early settlers were seeking rich farmland. Others wanted religious freedom. Settlers farmed, fished, and traded furs. In 1788, Connecticut became the fifth state to join the United States.

NATIVE PEOPLES OF CONNECTICUT

Today, five Native American groups that are recognized by the state or federal government remain in Connecticut.

MOHEGAN

- Original lands in southeastern Connecticut
- About 2,000 members today

MASHANTUCKET PEQUOT

- Original lands in southeastern Connecticut
- About 1,100 members today
- Also called Western Pequots

GOLDEN HILL PAUGUSSETT

- Original lands in the western half of Connecticut
- About 100 members today

EASTERN PEQUOT

- Original lands in southeastern Connecticut
- About 1,150 members today
- Also called Paucatuck

SCHAGHTICOKE

- Original lands in northwestern Connecticut
- About 300 members today

Highlands blanket both the western and eastern parts of Connecticut. At 2,380 feet (725 meters), Mount Frissell is the state's highest point. This mountain stands in Connecticut's northwest corner. The state's central lowlands cradle the

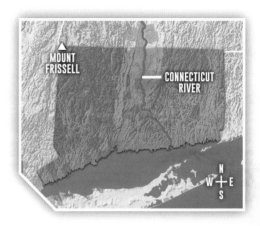

MOUNT FRISSELL

CONNECTICUT RIVER

N
W+E
S

Connecticut River valley. The river runs through the middle of the state. Forests cover more than half of Connecticut.

CONNECTICUT'S FUTURE: CLIMATE CHANGE

Scientists believe storms in Connecticut have been stronger in recent years due to climate change. This gradual changing of the weather will also bring more flooding and higher ocean levels. Connecticut's coast will face the greatest danger if this problem is not addressed.

CONNECTICUT RIVER

VIEW FROM MOUNT FRISSELL

SPRING
HIGH: 59°F (15°C)
LOW: 40°F (4°C)

SUMMER
HIGH: 81°F (27°C)
LOW: 62°F (17°C)

FALL
HIGH: 63°F (17°C)
LOW: 45°F (7°C)

WINTER
HIGH: 39°F (4°C)
LOW: 23°F (-5°C)

°F = degrees Fahrenheit
°C = degrees Celsius

RIVERS OF ICE

January of 2018 was a month of wild weather in Connecticut. Freezing temperatures, a quick thaw, and a rainstorm created huge ice jams on several rivers!

Connecticut's climate is **humid** and mild. **Precipitation** falls during all four seasons. Coastal storms called **nor'easters** bring heavy precipitation and strong winds. Snowstorms, flooding, and **hurricanes** also hit Connecticut.

11

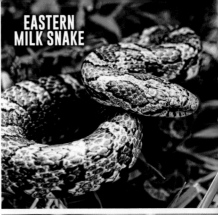

EASTERN MILK SNAKE

A wide variety of wildlife lives in Connecticut. In the northwestern hills, black bears roam in search of berries and bees. Bobcats hunt for squirrels, white-tailed deer, and rabbits. At nighttime, eastern milk snakes slither as brown bats dart about looking for insects. Muskrats swim in wetlands, feeding on plants, insects, snails, and fish.

MUSKRAT

High in the treetops, bald eagles take flight from nests. They often steal fish from gulls and ospreys along the coast. Loggerhead turtles glide through the waters of Long Island Sound.

BALD EAGLE

WHALE TALE

The sperm whale is the Connecticut state animal. It was chosen to remember Connecticut's whaling history.

LOGGERHEAD TURTLE

BOBCAT

Life Span: up to 15 years
Status: least concern

bobcat range = ▮

LEAST CONCERN	NEAR THREATENED	VULNERABLE	ENDANGERED	CRITICALLY ENDANGERED	EXTINCT IN THE WILD	EXTINCT
▲						

More than 3.6 million people live in Connecticut. The state's population is big for its size. Most Connecticuters live in towns and cities such as Bridgeport. Hartford, New Haven, and Stamford are also population centers.

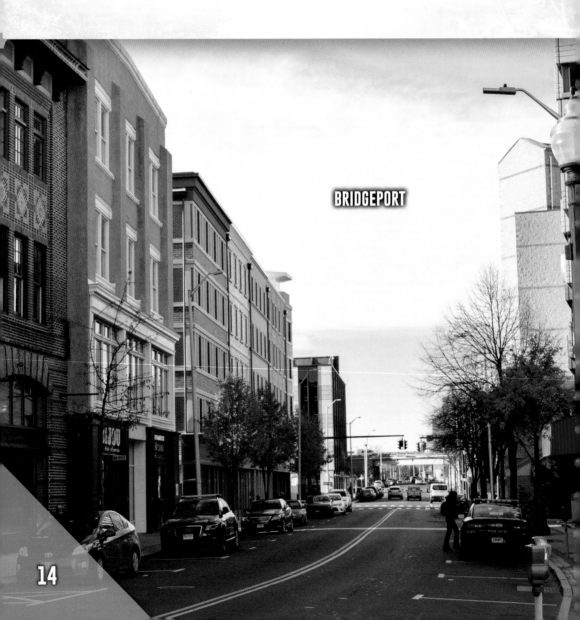

BRIDGEPORT

FAMOUS CONNECTICUTER

Name: Suzanne Collins

Born: August 10, 1962

Hometown: Hartford, Connecticut

Famous For: Award-winning author of the best-selling book series The Hunger Games

The majority of Connecticuters are of European **descent**. Hispanic and African American or Black people make up the next-largest groups. Many recent **immigrants** come from Asia, especially India and China. Fewer than 1 out of 100 people living in Connecticut is Native American.

STAMFORD

15

Hartford was founded in 1635 by a group of English colonists. The city's location on the Connecticut River has made it an important shipping port and trade center since colonial times. Hartford became the official state capital in 1875.

Thousands of students attend the city's many colleges and universities. Hartford residents visit the Wadsworth Atheneum to see the museum's 50,000 pieces of art. People also celebrate Hartford's rich **ethnic** communities. On Franklin Avenue, people enjoy tasty Italian pastries. Spanish-speaking businesses line Park Street, many of which offer delicious Latin American food.

A STORIED PAST

In the late 1800s, Hartford was one of the richest cities in the U.S. Famous residents included authors Mark Twain and Harriet Beecher Stowe.

WADSWORTH ATHENEUM

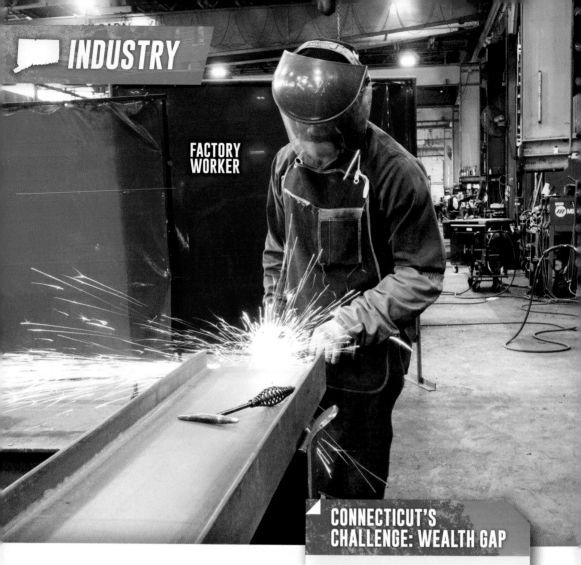

INDUSTRY

FACTORY WORKER

CONNECTICUT'S CHALLENGE: WEALTH GAP

Connecticut has one of the country's largest gaps between the state's richest and poorest people. Low-income families have fewer opportunities. Lessening the gap would help the state's economy grow and allow more people to thrive.

In its early days, most people in Connecticut made a living by farming. During the 1800s, **manufacturing** became much more important to the state's economy. Early factories produced goods such as silk, clocks, and guns. Today, factory workers make aircraft engines, computer parts, and products for the space industry.

Most people in Connecticut have **service jobs**. Some work in the **insurance** business or banks. Others have jobs in museums, schools, or hospitals. The state's farms produce dairy products, eggs, and garden plants. Some Connecticuters catch shellfish, such as lobsters, oysters, and clams. Fish farms also raise fish like branzino.

INVENTED IN CONNECTICUT

SPEED LIMIT 45

AUTOMOBILE SPEED LIMIT

Date Invented: submitted to State General Assembly in 1901
Inventor: Robert Woodruff

CAN OPENER

Date Patented: 1858
Inventor: Ezra J. Warner

POLAROID (INSTANT) CAMERA

Date Invented: 1947
Inventor: Edwin Land

WIFFLE BALL

Date Invented: 1953
Inventor: David N. Mullany

WHITE CLAM PIE

Connecticuters are serious about their food. Seafood is wildly popular. Favorite fish dishes include lobster rolls and a pizza called white clam pie. New Haven claims the first hamburgers in the United States were made there in 1900. Steamed cheeseburgers are a specialty from central Connecticut.

GIANT PEZ

PEZ candies are manufactured in Orange, Connecticut. The PEZ Visitor Center has the world's biggest dispenser. It is over 14 feet (4.3 meters) tall!

Connecticuters love their sweets. Connecticut's official state cookie is the snickerdoodle. Apple cider is a **traditional** Connecticut drink. The Foxon Park company has been making soda in East Haven since 1922! Unusual flavors include white birch and iron brew. Local dairies also serve sweets. Banana chocolate chip and blueberry cheesecake ice cream are favorites!

SNICKERDOODLES

APPLE CIDER

POUND CAKE

8 SERVINGS

Pound cake appears in a cookbook published in Hartford, Connecticut, back in 1795. It is rich and sweet. Have an adult help you make this recipe.

INGREDIENTS

1 cup (2 sticks) butter, softened

1 cup sugar

4 eggs

1 3/4 cups flour

cooking spray

DIRECTIONS

1. Preheat the oven to 350 degrees Fahrenheit (177 degrees Celsius).

2. In a big bowl, beat the sugar and butter together until the mixture is light and fluffy.

3. Add in the eggs, one at a time.

4. Gradually add the flour to the mixture until just combined.

5. Coat a 9-by-5-inch loaf pan with cooking spray. Pour in the batter.

6. Bake for about 1 hour. The cake is done when a toothpick stuck in the cake comes out clean.

7. Allow the cake to cool for 15 minutes, then tip onto a rack to cool completely. Enjoy!

SPORTS AND ENTERTAINMENT

BOATING

People love to boat and fish along Connecticut's coastline and waterways. They hike or camp in the state's parks and forests. Basketball is a very popular sport across Connecticut. Fans cheer on the professional women's basketball team, the Connecticut Sun. The University of Connecticut's basketball teams also have a huge following.

Art lovers explore Connecticut's many galleries. History fans enjoy visiting the Nathan Hale Homestead, the Mark Twain House, and Gillette Castle. Nature lovers often take drives in the autumn to check out the colorful **foliage**.

GILLETTE CASTLE

NOTABLE SPORTS TEAM

Connecticut Sun
Sport: Women's National Basketball Association
Started: 1999
Place of Play: Mohegan Sun Arena

FESTIVALS AND TRADITIONS

FEAST OF GREEN CORN
AND DANCE
MASHANTUCKET PEQUOT TRIBE

GREEN CORN FESTIVALS

Multiple Native American tribes celebrate the importance of corn to their people in summer festivals. Music, dance, and traditional foods are part of the festivals' fun.

Connecticuters celebrate in all seasons. Each February, people flock to the Ice Festival in Mystic. Festivalgoers see ice sculptures and an icebreaker ship. People enjoy live music, eat special foods, and play winter games. Many cities host maple sugar festivals in March.

Connecticut has a long **maritime** history. New London hosts Sailfest each summer. Visitors can see all kinds of boats. They also attend outdoor concerts, see fireworks displays, and go on thrilling rides. Connecticuters celebrate their beautiful state and its traditions all year long!

SAILFEST FIREWORKS

1788

Connecticut becomes the fifth state in the U.S.

1614

Adriaen Block is the first European explorer to arrive in the area

1636-37

The Pequot lose control of their native lands to English settlers in the Pequot War

1633

The first European settlement in Connecticut is founded at Windsor

1701

Yale University is founded

1848
Slavery ends in Connecticut

1974
Ella Grasso is the first woman to be elected governor in the country

2018
May brings tornadoes and hail that cause damage in many parts of the state

1983
The Mashantucket Pequot are recognized by the federal government, which allows the tribe to buy back their original tribal land

1917-1918
About 67,000 Connecticuters serve in World War I

Nicknames: Constitution State, Nutmeg State

Motto: *Qui Transtulit Sustinet*
(He Who Transplanted Still Sustains)

Date of Statehood: January 9, 1788 (the 5th state)

Capital City: Hartford ★

Other Major Cities: Bridgeport, New Haven, Stamford

Area: 5,543 square miles (14,356 square kilometers); Connecticut is the 3rd smallest state.

Population

3,605,944
(2020)

STATE FLAG

The background of the Connecticut flag is blue. In the middle is a white coat of arms with three grapevines on it. Some say these represent Windsor, Hartford, and Wethersfield, the oldest settlements in the state. The state motto is located beneath the coat of arms.

INDUSTRY

Main Exports

JOBS

- MANUFACTURING **7%**
- FARMING AND NATURAL RESOURCES **1%**
- GOVERNMENT **11%**
- SERVICES **81%**

machinery

chemicals

transportation equipment

Natural Resources
forests, fertile soil, sand, gravel

GOVERNMENT

7 ELECTORAL VOTES

Federal Government
5 REPRESENTATIVES | **2** SENATORS

CT

USA

State Government
151 REPRESENTATIVES | **36** SENATORS

STATE SYMBOLS

STATE BIRD
AMERICAN ROBIN

STATE ANIMAL
SPERM WHALE

STATE FLOWER
MOUNTAIN LAUREL

STATE TREE
CHARTER OAK

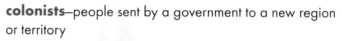

colonists—people sent by a government to a new region or territory

descent—background or ancestry

ethnic—related to a group of people who share customs and an identity

foliage—the leaves of a plant or of many plants

furl—to roll or wrap up around something

humid—having a lot of moisture in the air

hurricanes—storms formed in the tropics that have violent winds and often have rain and lightning

immigrants—people who move to a new country

insurance—a business in which people pay money for protection against injuries or damages

manufacturing—a field of work in which people use machines to make products

marina—a dock or basin where boats are anchored

maritime—relating to navigation or trade on the sea

New England—an area in the northeastern United States that includes Maine, New Hampshire, Vermont, Massachusetts, Rhode Island, and Connecticut

nor'easters—large storms that hit coastal northeastern states; winds blow in from the northeast.

precipitation—water that falls to the earth as rain, snow, sleet, mist, or hail

service jobs—jobs that perform tasks for people or businesses

settlements—places where newly arrived people live

sound—a long waterway separating a mainland and an island or connecting two larger bodies of water

traditional—related to customs, ideas, or beliefs handed down from one generation to the next

TO LEARN MORE

AT THE LIBRARY

Miller, Derek, Michael Burgan, Stephanie Fitzgerald, and Gerry Boehme. *Connecticut.* New York, N.Y.: Cavendish Square, 2020.

Rau, Dana Meachen. *Who Was Harriet Beecher Stowe?* New York, N.Y.: Grosset & Dunlap, 2015.

Tieck, Sarah. *Connecticut.* Minneapolis, Minn.: Abdo, 2020.

ON THE WEB

FACTSURFER

Factsurfer.com gives you a safe, fun way to find more information.

1. Go to www.factsurfer.com.

2. Enter "Connecticut" into the search box and click 🔍.

3. Select your book cover to see a list of related content.

INDEX

The images in this book are reproduced through the courtesy of: f11photo, front cover, pp. 2-3; Danny Smythe, pp. 3, 26; AlanHayes.com/ Alamy, pp. 4-5; Stan Tess/ Alamy, p. 5 (Dinosaur State Park); Sean Pavone, p. 5 (Mark Twain House); agefotostock/ Alamy, pp. 5 (Sleeping Giant State Park, Stewart B. McKinney National Wildlife Refuge), 11 (top); Pacific Press/ Agency/ Alamy, p. 8; Isabel Eve, p. 9; Jennifer Yakey-Ault, p. 10; Spencer Platt/ Staff/ Getty Images, p. 11 (bottom left); Enfi, p. 11 (bottom right); wildestanimal, p. 12 (sperm whale); Malachi Jacobs, p. 12 (milk snake); Toni Genes, p. 12 (muskrat); Chris Hill, p. 12 (eagle); Charlie Reaney, p. 12 (loggerhead turtle); Holly Kuchera, p. 13; Wendell Guy, p. 14; Anton_Ivanov, p. 15 (top); Christopher Halloran, p. 15 (middle); Richard A. McGuirk, p. 15 (bottom); Jacob Boomsma, p. 16; Zuri Swimmer/ Alamy, p. 17; Rachid Jalayanadeja, p. 18; Brent Hofacker, pp. 19 (speed limit), 21 (cider); Fluid Shutter, p. 19 (can opener); Anton Starikov/ Alamy, p. 19 (Polaroid); kelpfish, p. 19 (wiffle ball); George Oze/ Alamy, p. 19 (bottom); Heidi Besen, p. 20 (top); Sean Wandzilak, p. 20 (bottom); Ildi Papp, p. 21 (snickerdoodles); timquo, p. 21 (pound cake); MSPhotographic, p. 21 (background); Allan Wood Photography, p. 22; Karen Grigoryan, p. 23 (top); Hartford Courant/ Contributor/ Getty Images, p. 23 (middle); Lightspring, p. 23 (bottom); Miro Vrlik Photography/ Alamy, p. 24; Newspaper Member/ AP Images, p. 25; Bettmann/ Contributor/ Getty Images, p. 27; Mircea Costina, p. 29 (American robin); Shane Gross, p. 29 (sperm whale); jadimages, p. 29 (mountain laurel); Wadsworth Atheneum/ Wikipedia, p. 29 (Charter Oak); Jon Bilous, p. 31.